JIU-JITSU TRAINING JOURNAL AND LOG BOOK

THIS BOOK BELONGS TO:

Daniel Bourdages 780 991 4442

258 lbs

SESSION 1

wed
class

DATE: Jan 17/2024   BELT RANK: White ∅

INSTRUCTOR: Prof. Connor.   WEIGHT:

TRAINING PARTNERS: Steve, Thomas.

SESSION GOAL: Side Control Escapes.

TECHNIQUE 1

- Kesa Gatame Escape.
    - Elbow in - make Space
    - get Knees in Create "Frame"
    - half Guard.

TECHNIQUE 2

TECHNIQUE 3

NOTES

*Free Roll w/ Thomas - good Roll, Controlled Breathing, Calmed my movements.
*Free Roll w/ Steve - Very strong, I with Stood the barge, was in Bottom Position till I performed Sweep. *When Someone is Constrating on Technique, good time to Perform an Escape.

RATING

1	2	3	4	5	6	7	8	9	10
☐	☐	☐	☐	☒	☐	☐	☐	☐	☐

+ Good Control of Breathing
+ Resistance Band walks "green"
- need Better flexibility

MINUTES TRAINED: 60min

SESSION 2

DATE:_____ BELT RANK:_____

INSTRUCTOR:_____ WEIGHT:_____

TRAINING PARTNERS:_____

SESSION GOAL:_____

TECHNIQUE 1

_____
_____
_____
_____
_____
_____
_____

TECHNIQUE 2

_____
_____
_____
_____
_____
_____
_____

TECHNIQUE 3

_____

_____

_____

_____

_____

_____

_____

_____

NOTES

_____

_____

_____

_____

_____

_____

_____

RATING

1	2	3	4	5	6	7	8	9	10
☐	☐	☐	☐	☐	☐	☐	☐	☐	☐

MINUTES TRAINED: _____

SESSION 3

DATE:_____   BELT RANK:_____

INSTRUCTOR:_____   WEIGHT:_____

TRAINING PARTNERS:_____

SESSION GOAL:_____

TECHNIQUE 1

_____

_____

_____

_____

_____

_____

_____

TECHNIQUE 2

_____

_____

_____

_____

_____

_____

_____

TECHNIQUE 3

_____

_____

_____

_____

_____

_____

_____

_____

NOTES

_____

_____

_____

_____

_____

_____

_____

_____

RATING

1	2	3	4	5	6	7	8	9	10
☐	☐	☐	☐	☐	☐	☐	☐	☐	☐

MINUTES TRAINED: _____

SESSION 4

DATE:_____ BELT RANK:_____

INSTRUCTOR:_____ WEIGHT:_____

TRAINING PARTNERS:_____

SESSION GOAL:_____

TECHNIQUE 1

_____

_____

_____

_____

_____

_____

_____

TECHNIQUE 2

_____

_____

_____

_____

_____

_____

_____

TECHNIQUE 3

_____

_____

_____

_____

_____

_____

_____

_____

NOTES

_____

_____

_____

_____

_____

_____

_____

_____

RATING

1	2	3	4	5	6	7	8	9	10
☐	☐	☐	☐	☐	☐	☐	☐	☐	☐

MINUTES TRAINED: _____

SESSION 5

DATE:_____ BELT RANK:_____

INSTRUCTOR:_____ WEIGHT:_____

TRAINING PARTNERS:_____

SESSION GOAL:_____

TECHNIQUE 1

_____

_____

_____

_____

_____

_____

_____

TECHNIQUE 2

_____

_____

_____

_____

_____

_____

_____

TECHNIQUE 3

_____

_____

_____

_____

_____

_____

_____

_____

NOTES

_____

_____

_____

_____

_____

_____

_____

_____

RATING

1	2	3	4	5	6	7	8	9	10
☐	☐	☐	☐	☐	☐	☐	☐	☐	☐

MINUTES TRAINED: _____

SESSION 6

DATE:_____   BELT RANK:_____

INSTRUCTOR: _____   WEIGHT:_____

TRAINING PARTNERS: _____

SESSION GOAL:_____

TECHNIQUE 1

_____

_____

_____

_____

_____

_____

_____

TECHNIQUE 2

_____

_____

_____

_____

_____

_____

_____

TECHNIQUE 3

_____

_____

_____

_____

_____

_____

_____

_____

NOTES

_____

_____

_____

_____

_____

_____

_____

_____

RATING

1	2	3	4	5	6	7	8	9	10
☐	☐	☐	☐	☐	☐	☐	☐	☐	☐

MINUTES TRAINED: _____

SESSION 7

DATE:_____   BELT RANK:_____

INSTRUCTOR:_____   WEIGHT:_____

TRAINING PARTNERS:_____

SESSION GOAL:_____

TECHNIQUE 1

_____
_____
_____
_____
_____
_____
_____

TECHNIQUE 2

_____
_____
_____
_____
_____
_____
_____

TECHNIQUE 3

_____

_____

_____

_____

_____

_____

_____

_____

NOTES

_____

_____

_____

_____

_____

_____

_____

_____

RATING

1	2	3	4	5	6	7	8	9	10
☐	☐	☐	☐	☐	☐	☐	☐	☐	☐

MINUTES TRAINED: _____

SESSION 8

DATE:_____   BELT RANK:_____

INSTRUCTOR:_____   WEIGHT:_____

TRAINING PARTNERS:_____

SESSION GOAL:_____

TECHNIQUE 1

_____

_____

_____

_____

_____

_____

_____

TECHNIQUE 2

_____

_____

_____

_____

_____

_____

_____

TECHNIQUE 3

_____

_____

_____

_____

_____

_____

_____

NOTES

_____

_____

_____

_____

_____

_____

_____

RATING

1	2	3	4	5	6	7	8	9	10
☐	☐	☐	☐	☐	☐	☐	☐	☐	☐

MINUTES TRAINED: _____

SESSION 9

DATE:_____   BELT RANK:_____

INSTRUCTOR:_____   WEIGHT:_____

TRAINING PARTNERS: _____

SESSION GOAL:_____

TECHNIQUE 1

_____

_____

_____

_____

_____

_____

_____

TECHNIQUE 2

_____

_____

_____

_____

_____

_____

_____

TECHNIQUE 3

_____

_____

_____

_____

_____

_____

_____

_____

NOTES

_____

_____

_____

_____

_____

_____

_____

_____

RATING

1	2	3	4	5	6	7	8	9	10
☐	☐	☐	☐	☐	☐	☐	☐	☐	☐

MINUTES TRAINED: _____

SESSION 10

DATE:_____   BELT RANK:_____

INSTRUCTOR:_____   WEIGHT:_____

TRAINING PARTNERS:_____

SESSION GOAL:_____

TECHNIQUE 1

_____
_____
_____
_____
_____
_____
_____

TECHNIQUE 2

_____
_____
_____
_____
_____
_____

TECHNIQUE 3

_____
_____
_____
_____
_____
_____
_____
_____

NOTES

_____
_____
_____
_____
_____
_____
_____
_____

RATING

1	2	3	4	5	6	7	8	9	10
☐	☐	☐	☐	☐	☐	☐	☐	☐	☐

MINUTES TRAINED: _____

SESSION 11

DATE:_____   BELT RANK:_____

INSTRUCTOR:_____   WEIGHT:_____

TRAINING PARTNERS:_____

SESSION GOAL:_____

TECHNIQUE 1

_____

_____

_____

_____

_____

_____

_____

TECHNIQUE 2

_____

_____

_____

_____

_____

_____

_____

TECHNIQUE 3

_____

_____

_____

_____

_____

_____

_____

NOTES

_____

_____

_____

_____

_____

_____

_____

RATING

1	2	3	4	5	6	7	8	9	10
☐	☐	☐	☐	☐	☐	☐	☐	☐	☐

MINUTES TRAINED: _____

SESSION 12

DATE:_____   BELT RANK:_____

INSTRUCTOR:_____   WEIGHT:_____

TRAINING PARTNERS:_____

SESSION GOAL:_____

TECHNIQUE 1

_____

_____

_____

_____

_____

_____

_____

TECHNIQUE 2

_____

_____

_____

_____

_____

_____

_____

TECHNIQUE 3

_____

_____

_____

_____

_____

_____

_____

_____

NOTES

_____

_____

_____

_____

_____

_____

_____

_____

RATING

1	2	3	4	5	6	7	8	9	10
☐	☐	☐	☐	☐	☐	☐	☐	☐	☐

MINUTES TRAINED: _____

SESSION 13

DATE:_____   BELT RANK:_____

INSTRUCTOR:_____   WEIGHT:_____

TRAINING PARTNERS:_____

SESSION GOAL:_____

TECHNIQUE 1

_____

_____

_____

_____

_____

_____

_____

TECHNIQUE 2

_____

_____

_____

_____

_____

_____

_____

TECHNIQUE 3

_____

_____

_____

_____

_____

_____

_____

_____

NOTES

_____

_____

_____

_____

_____

_____

_____

_____

RATING

1	2	3	4	5	6	7	8	9	10
☐	☐	☐	☐	☐	☐	☐	☐	☐	☐

MINUTES TRAINED: _____

SESSION 14

DATE:_____   BELT RANK:_____

INSTRUCTOR:_____   WEIGHT:_____

TRAINING PARTNERS:_____

SESSION GOAL:_____

TECHNIQUE 1

_____

_____

_____

_____

_____

_____

_____

TECHNIQUE 2

_____

_____

_____

_____

_____

_____

_____

TECHNIQUE 3

_____

_____

_____

_____

_____

_____

_____

NOTES

_____

_____

_____

_____

_____

_____

_____

RATING

1	2	3	4	5	6	7	8	9	10
☐	☐	☐	☐	☐	☐	☐	☐	☐	☐

MINUTES TRAINED: _____

SESSION 15

DATE:_____   BELT RANK:_____

INSTRUCTOR:_____   WEIGHT:_____

TRAINING PARTNERS:_____

SESSION GOAL:_____

TECHNIQUE 1

_____

_____

_____

_____

_____

_____

_____

TECHNIQUE 2

_____

_____

_____

_____

_____

_____

_____

TECHNIQUE 3

_____
_____
_____
_____
_____
_____
_____
_____

NOTES

_____
_____
_____
_____
_____
_____
_____
_____

RATING

1	2	3	4	5	6	7	8	9	10
☐	☐	☐	☐	☐	☐	☐	☐	☐	☐

MINUTES TRAINED: _____

SESSION 16

DATE:_____   BELT RANK:_____

INSTRUCTOR:_____   WEIGHT:_____

TRAINING PARTNERS:_____

SESSION GOAL:_____

TECHNIQUE 1

_____

_____

_____

_____

_____

_____

_____

TECHNIQUE 2

_____

_____

_____

_____

_____

_____

_____

TECHNIQUE 3

_____

_____

_____

_____

_____

_____

_____

NOTES

_____

_____

_____

_____

_____

_____

_____

RATING

1	2	3	4	5	6	7	8	9	10
☐	☐	☐	☐	☐	☐	☐	☐	☐	☐

MINUTES TRAINED: _____

SESSION 17

DATE:_____   BELT RANK:_____

INSTRUCTOR:_____   WEIGHT:_____

TRAINING PARTNERS:_____

SESSION GOAL:_____

TECHNIQUE 1

_____
_____
_____
_____
_____
_____
_____

TECHNIQUE 2

_____
_____
_____
_____
_____
_____
_____

TECHNIQUE 3

_____

_____

_____

_____

_____

_____

_____

_____

NOTES

_____

_____

_____

_____

_____

_____

_____

_____

RATING

1	2	3	4	5	6	7	8	9	10
☐	☐	☐	☐	☐	☐	☐	☐	☐	☐

MINUTES TRAINED: _____

SESSION 18

DATE:_____   BELT RANK:_____

INSTRUCTOR:_____   WEIGHT:_____

TRAINING PARTNERS:_____

SESSION GOAL:_____

TECHNIQUE 1

_____

_____

_____

_____

_____

_____

_____

TECHNIQUE 2

_____

_____

_____

_____

_____

_____

_____

TECHNIQUE 3

_____

_____

_____

_____

_____

_____

_____

_____

NOTES

_____

_____

_____

_____

_____

_____

_____

_____

RATING

1	2	3	4	5	6	7	8	9	10
☐	☐	☐	☐	☐	☐	☐	☐	☐	☐

MINUTES TRAINED: _____

SESSION 19

DATE:_____   BELT RANK:_____

INSTRUCTOR:_____   WEIGHT:_____

TRAINING PARTNERS:_____

SESSION GOAL:_____

TECHNIQUE 1

_____

_____

_____

_____

_____

_____

_____

TECHNIQUE 2

_____

_____

_____

_____

_____

_____

_____

_____

_____

_____

_____

_____

_____

_____

NOTES

_____

_____

_____

_____

_____

_____

_____

RATING

1	2	3	4	5	6	7	8	9	10
☐	☐	☐	☐	☐	☐	☐	☐	☐	☐

MINUTES TRAINED: _____

SESSION 20

DATE:_____ BELT RANK:_____

INSTRUCTOR:_____ WEIGHT:_____

TRAINING PARTNERS:_____

SESSION GOAL:_____

TECHNIQUE 1

_____

_____

_____

_____

_____

_____

_____

TECHNIQUE 2

_____

_____

_____

_____

_____

_____

_____

TECHNIQUE 3

_____

_____

_____

_____

_____

_____

_____

NOTES

_____

_____

_____

_____

_____

_____

_____

RATING

1	2	3	4	5	6	7	8	9	10
☐	☐	☐	☐	☐	☐	☐	☐	☐	☐

MINUTES TRAINED: _____

SESSION 21

DATE:_____   BELT RANK:_____

INSTRUCTOR:_____   WEIGHT:_____

TRAINING PARTNERS:_____

SESSION GOAL:_____

TECHNIQUE 1

_____
_____
_____
_____
_____
_____
_____

TECHNIQUE 2

_____
_____
_____
_____
_____
_____
_____

TECHNIQUE 3

_____

_____

_____

_____

_____

_____

_____

NOTES

_____

_____

_____

_____

_____

_____

_____

RATING

1	2	3	4	5	6	7	8	9	10
☐	☐	☐	☐	☐	☐	☐	☐	☐	☐

MINUTES TRAINED: _____

SESSION 22

DATE:_____   BELT RANK:_____

INSTRUCTOR:_____   WEIGHT:_____

TRAINING PARTNERS:_____

SESSION GOAL:_____

TECHNIQUE 1

_____

_____

_____

_____

_____

_____

_____

TECHNIQUE 2

_____

_____

_____

_____

_____

_____

_____

TECHNIQUE 3

_____

_____

_____

_____

_____

_____

_____

NOTES

_____

_____

_____

_____

_____

_____

_____

RATING

1	2	3	4	5	6	7	8	9	10
☐	☐	☐	☐	☐	☐	☐	☐	☐	☐

MINUTES TRAINED: _____

SESSION 23

DATE:_____   BELT RANK:_____

INSTRUCTOR:_____   WEIGHT:_____

TRAINING PARTNERS:_____

SESSION GOAL:_____

TECHNIQUE 1

_____
_____
_____
_____
_____
_____
_____

TECHNIQUE 2

_____
_____
_____
_____
_____
_____
_____

TECHNIQUE 3

_____

_____

_____

_____

_____

_____

_____

_____

NOTES

_____

_____

_____

_____

_____

_____

_____

_____

RATING

1	2	3	4	5	6	7	8	9	10
☐	☐	☐	☐	☐	☐	☐	☐	☐	☐

MINUTES TRAINED: _____

SESSION 24

DATE:_____   BELT RANK:_____

INSTRUCTOR:_____   WEIGHT:_____

TRAINING PARTNERS:_____

SESSION GOAL:_____

TECHNIQUE 1

_____
_____
_____
_____
_____
_____
_____

TECHNIQUE 2

_____
_____
_____
_____
_____
_____
_____

TECHNIQUE 3

_____

_____

_____

_____

_____

_____

_____

NOTES

_____

_____

_____

_____

_____

_____

_____

RATING

1	2	3	4	5	6	7	8	9	10
☐	☐	☐	☐	☐	☐	☐	☐	☐	☐

MINUTES TRAINED: _____

SESSION 25

DATE:_____   BELT RANK:_____

INSTRUCTOR:_____   WEIGHT:_____

TRAINING PARTNERS:_____

SESSION GOAL:_____

TECHNIQUE 1

_____
_____
_____
_____
_____
_____
_____

TECHNIQUE 2

_____
_____
_____
_____
_____
_____
_____

TECHNIQUE 3

_____

_____

_____

_____

_____

_____

_____

NOTES

_____

_____

_____

_____

_____

_____

_____

RATING

1	2	3	4	5	6	7	8	9	10
☐	☐	☐	☐	☐	☐	☐	☐	☐	☐

MINUTES TRAINED: _____

SESSION 26

DATE:_____   BELT RANK:_____

INSTRUCTOR:_____   WEIGHT:_____

TRAINING PARTNERS:_____

SESSION GOAL:_____

TECHNIQUE 1

_____

_____

_____

_____

_____

_____

_____

TECHNIQUE 2

_____

_____

_____

_____

_____

_____

_____

TECHNIQUE 3

_____

_____

_____

_____

_____

_____

_____

NOTES

_____

_____

_____

_____

_____

_____

_____

RATING

1	2	3	4	5	6	7	8	9	10
☐	☐	☐	☐	☐	☐	☐	☐	☐	☐

MINUTES TRAINED: _____

SESSION 27

DATE:_____   BELT RANK:_____

INSTRUCTOR:_____   WEIGHT:_____

TRAINING PARTNERS:_____

SESSION GOAL:_____

TECHNIQUE 1

_____

_____

_____

_____

_____

_____

_____

TECHNIQUE 2

_____

_____

_____

_____

_____

_____

_____

TECHNIQUE 3

_____

_____

_____

_____

_____

_____

_____

NOTES

_____

_____

_____

_____

_____

_____

_____

RATING

1	2	3	4	5	6	7	8	9	10
☐	☐	☐	☐	☐	☐	☐	☐	☐	☐

MINUTES TRAINED: _____

SESSION 28

DATE:_____   BELT RANK:_____

INSTRUCTOR:_____   WEIGHT:_____

TRAINING PARTNERS:_____

SESSION GOAL:_____

TECHNIQUE 1

_____

_____

_____

_____

_____

_____

_____

TECHNIQUE 2

_____

_____

_____

_____

_____

_____

_____

TECHNIQUE 3

_____

_____

_____

_____

_____

_____

_____

NOTES

_____

_____

_____

_____

_____

_____

_____

RATING

1	2	3	4	5	6	7	8	9	10
☐	☐	☐	☐	☐	☐	☐	☐	☐	☐

MINUTES TRAINED: _____

SESSION 29

DATE:_____   BELT RANK:_____

INSTRUCTOR:_____   WEIGHT:_____

TRAINING PARTNERS:_____

SESSION GOAL:_____

TECHNIQUE 1

_____

_____

_____

_____

_____

_____

_____

TECHNIQUE 2

_____

_____

_____

_____

_____

_____

_____

TECHNIQUE 3

_____

_____

_____

_____

_____

_____

_____

NOTES

_____

_____

_____

_____

_____

_____

_____

RATING

1	2	3	4	5	6	7	8	9	10
☐	☐	☐	☐	☐	☐	☐	☐	☐	☐

MINUTES TRAINED: _____

SESSION 30

DATE:_____ BELT RANK:_____

INSTRUCTOR:_____ WEIGHT:_____

TRAINING PARTNERS:_____

SESSION GOAL:_____

TECHNIQUE 1

_____
_____
_____
_____
_____
_____
_____

TECHNIQUE 2

_____
_____
_____
_____
_____
_____
_____

TECHNIQUE 3

_____

_____

_____

_____

_____

_____

_____

NOTES

_____

_____

_____

_____

_____

_____

_____

RATING

1	2	3	4	5	6	7	8	9	10
☐	☐	☐	☐	☐	☐	☐	☐	☐	☐

MINUTES TRAINED: _____

SESSION 31

DATE:_____   BELT RANK:_____

INSTRUCTOR:_____   WEIGHT:_____

TRAINING PARTNERS:_____

SESSION GOAL:_____

TECHNIQUE 1

_____

_____

_____

_____

_____

_____

_____

TECHNIQUE 2

_____

_____

_____

_____

_____

_____

_____

TECHNIQUE 3

_____

_____

_____

_____

_____

_____

_____

NOTES

_____

_____

_____

_____

_____

_____

_____

_____

RATING

1	2	3	4	5	6	7	8	9	10
☐	☐	☐	☐	☐	☐	☐	☐	☐	☐

MINUTES TRAINED: _____

SESSION 32

DATE:_____   BELT RANK:_____

INSTRUCTOR:_____   WEIGHT:_____

TRAINING PARTNERS:_____

SESSION GOAL:_____

TECHNIQUE 1

_____

_____

_____

_____

_____

_____

_____

TECHNIQUE 2

_____

_____

_____

_____

_____

_____

_____

TECHNIQUE 3

_____

_____

_____

_____

_____

_____

_____

_____

NOTES

_____

_____

_____

_____

_____

_____

_____

_____

RATING

1	2	3	4	5	6	7	8	9	10
☐	☐	☐	☐	☐	☐	☐	☐	☐	☐

MINUTES TRAINED: _____

SESSION 33

DATE:_____   BELT RANK:_____

INSTRUCTOR:_____   WEIGHT:_____

TRAINING PARTNERS:_____

SESSION GOAL:_____

TECHNIQUE 1

_____

_____

_____

_____

_____

_____

_____

TECHNIQUE 2

_____

_____

_____

_____

_____

_____

_____

TECHNIQUE 3

_____

_____

_____

_____

_____

_____

_____

NOTES

_____

_____

_____

_____

_____

_____

_____

_____

RATING

1	2	3	4	5	6	7	8	9	10
☐	☐	☐	☐	☐	☐	☐	☐	☐	☐

MINUTES TRAINED: _____

SESSION 34

DATE:_____   BELT RANK:_____

INSTRUCTOR:_____   WEIGHT:_____

TRAINING PARTNERS:_____

SESSION GOAL:_____

TECHNIQUE 1

_____

_____

_____

_____

_____

_____

_____

TECHNIQUE 2

_____

_____

_____

_____

_____

_____

_____

TECHNIQUE 3

_____

_____

_____

_____

_____

_____

_____

NOTES

_____

_____

_____

_____

_____

_____

_____

RATING

1	2	3	4	5	6	7	8	9	10
☐	☐	☐	☐	☐	☐	☐	☐	☐	☐

MINUTES TRAINED: _____

SESSION 35

DATE:_____   BELT RANK:_____

INSTRUCTOR:_____   WEIGHT:_____

TRAINING PARTNERS:_____

SESSION GOAL:_____

TECHNIQUE 1

_____
_____
_____
_____
_____
_____
_____

TECHNIQUE 2

_____
_____
_____
_____
_____
_____
_____

TECHNIQUE 3

_____

_____

_____

_____

_____

_____

_____

NOTES

_____

_____

_____

_____

_____

_____

_____

RATING

1	2	3	4	5	6	7	8	9	10
☐	☐	☐	☐	☐	☐	☐	☐	☐	☐

MINUTES TRAINED: _____

SESSION 36

DATE:_____   BELT RANK:_____

INSTRUCTOR:_____   WEIGHT:_____

TRAINING PARTNERS:_____

SESSION GOAL:_____

TECHNIQUE 1

_____

_____

_____

_____

_____

_____

_____

TECHNIQUE 2

_____

_____

_____

_____

_____

_____

_____

TECHNIQUE 3

_____

_____

_____

_____

_____

_____

_____

NOTES

_____

_____

_____

_____

_____

_____

_____

_____

RATING

1	2	3	4	5	6	7	8	9	10
☐	☐	☐	☐	☐	☐	☐	☐	☐	☐

MINUTES TRAINED: _____

SESSION 37

DATE:_____   BELT RANK:_____

INSTRUCTOR:_____   WEIGHT:_____

TRAINING PARTNERS:_____

SESSION GOAL:_____

TECHNIQUE 1

_____

_____

_____

_____

_____

_____

_____

TECHNIQUE 2

_____

_____

_____

_____

_____

_____

_____

TECHNIQUE 3

_____

_____

_____

_____

_____

_____

_____

NOTES

_____

_____

_____

_____

_____

_____

_____

RATING

1	2	3	4	5	6	7	8	9	10
☐	☐	☐	☐	☐	☐	☐	☐	☐	☐

MINUTES TRAINED: _____

SESSION 38

DATE:_____   BELT RANK:_____

INSTRUCTOR:_____   WEIGHT:_____

TRAINING PARTNERS:_____

SESSION GOAL:_____

TECHNIQUE 1

_____

_____

_____

_____

_____

_____

_____

TECHNIQUE 2

_____

_____

_____

_____

_____

_____

_____

TECHNIQUE 3

_____

_____

_____

_____

_____

_____

_____

NOTES

_____

_____

_____

_____

_____

_____

_____

RATING

1	2	3	4	5	6	7	8	9	10
☐	☐	☐	☐	☐	☐	☐	☐	☐	☐

MINUTES TRAINED: _____

SESSION 39

DATE:_____   BELT RANK:_____

INSTRUCTOR:_____   WEIGHT:_____

TRAINING PARTNERS:_____

SESSION GOAL:_____

TECHNIQUE 1

_____

_____

_____

_____

_____

_____

_____

TECHNIQUE 2

_____

_____

_____

_____

_____

_____

_____

TECHNIQUE 3

_____

_____

_____

_____

_____

_____

_____

NOTES

_____

_____

_____

_____

_____

_____

_____

RATING

1	2	3	4	5	6	7	8	9	10
☐	☐	☐	☐	☐	☐	☐	☐	☐	☐

MINUTES TRAINED: _____

SESSION 40

DATE:_____   BELT RANK:_____

INSTRUCTOR:_____   WEIGHT:_____

TRAINING PARTNERS:_____

SESSION GOAL:_____

TECHNIQUE 1

_____

_____

_____

_____

_____

_____

_____

TECHNIQUE 2

_____

_____

_____

_____

_____

_____

_____

TECHNIQUE 3

_____

_____

_____

_____

_____

_____

_____

NOTES

_____

_____

_____

_____

_____

_____

_____

_____

RATING

1	2	3	4	5	6	7	8	9	10
☐	☐	☐	☐	☐	☐	☐	☐	☐	☐

MINUTES TRAINED: _____

SESSION 41

DATE:_____   BELT RANK:_____

INSTRUCTOR:_____   WEIGHT:_____

TRAINING PARTNERS: _____

SESSION GOAL:_____

TECHNIQUE 1

_____
_____
_____
_____
_____
_____
_____

TECHNIQUE 2

_____
_____
_____
_____
_____
_____
_____

TECHNIQUE 3

_____

_____

_____

_____

_____

_____

_____

NOTES

_____

_____

_____

_____

_____

_____

_____

RATING

1	2	3	4	5	6	7	8	9	10
☐	☐	☐	☐	☐	☐	☐	☐	☐	☐

MINUTES TRAINED: _____

SESSION 42

DATE:_____   BELT RANK:_____

INSTRUCTOR:_____   WEIGHT:_____

TRAINING PARTNERS: _____

SESSION GOAL:_____

TECHNIQUE 1

_____

_____

_____

_____

_____

_____

_____

TECHNIQUE 2

_____

_____

_____

_____

_____

_____

_____

TECHNIQUE 3

_____

_____

_____

_____

_____

_____

_____

NOTES

_____

_____

_____

_____

_____

_____

_____

RATING

1	2	3	4	5	6	7	8	9	10
☐	☐	☐	☐	☐	☐	☐	☐	☐	☐

MINUTES TRAINED: _____

SESSION 43

DATE:_____   BELT RANK:_____

INSTRUCTOR:_____   WEIGHT:_____

TRAINING PARTNERS:_____

SESSION GOAL:_____

TECHNIQUE 1

_____

_____

_____

_____

_____

_____

_____

TECHNIQUE 2

_____

_____

_____

_____

_____

_____

_____

TECHNIQUE 3

_____

_____

_____

_____

_____

_____

_____

NOTES

_____

_____

_____

_____

_____

_____

_____

RATING

1	2	3	4	5	6	7	8	9	10
☐	☐	☐	☐	☐	☐	☐	☐	☐	☐

MINUTES TRAINED: _____

SESSION 44

DATE:_____   BELT RANK:_____

INSTRUCTOR:_____   WEIGHT:_____

TRAINING PARTNERS:_____

SESSION GOAL:_____

TECHNIQUE 1

_____

_____

_____

_____

_____

_____

_____

TECHNIQUE 2

_____

_____

_____

_____

_____

_____

_____

TECHNIQUE 3

_____

_____

_____

_____

_____

_____

_____

NOTES

_____

_____

_____

_____

_____

_____

_____

RATING

1	2	3	4	5	6	7	8	9	10
☐	☐	☐	☐	☐	☐	☐	☐	☐	☐

MINUTES TRAINED: _____

SESSION 45

DATE:_____   BELT RANK:_____

INSTRUCTOR:_____   WEIGHT:_____

TRAINING PARTNERS: _____

SESSION GOAL:_____

TECHNIQUE 1

_____

_____

_____

_____

_____

_____

_____

TECHNIQUE 2

_____

_____

_____

_____

_____

_____

_____

TECHNIQUE 3

_____

_____

_____

_____

_____

_____

_____

NOTES

_____

_____

_____

_____

_____

_____

_____

RATING

1	2	3	4	5	6	7	8	9	10
☐	☐	☐	☐	☐	☐	☐	☐	☐	☐

MINUTES TRAINED: _____

SESSION 46

DATE:_____   BELT RANK:_____

INSTRUCTOR:_____   WEIGHT:_____

TRAINING PARTNERS:_____

SESSION GOAL:_____

TECHNIQUE 1

_____

_____

_____

_____

_____

_____

_____

TECHNIQUE 2

_____

_____

_____

_____

_____

_____

_____

TECHNIQUE 3

_____

_____

_____

_____

_____

_____

_____

NOTES

_____

_____

_____

_____

_____

_____

_____

RATING

1	2	3	4	5	6	7	8	9	10
☐	☐	☐	☐	☐	☐	☐	☐	☐	☐

MINUTES TRAINED: _____

SESSION 47

DATE:_____   BELT RANK:_____

INSTRUCTOR:_____   WEIGHT:_____

TRAINING PARTNERS:_____

SESSION GOAL:_____

TECHNIQUE 1

_____

_____

_____

_____

_____

_____

_____

TECHNIQUE 2

_____

_____

_____

_____

_____

_____

TECHNIQUE 3

_____

_____

_____

_____

_____

_____

_____

NOTES

_____

_____

_____

_____

_____

_____

_____

RATING

1	2	3	4	5	6	7	8	9	10
☐	☐	☐	☐	☐	☐	☐	☐	☐	☐

MINUTES TRAINED: _____

SESSION 48

DATE:_____   BELT RANK:_____

INSTRUCTOR:_____   WEIGHT:_____

TRAINING PARTNERS:_____

SESSION GOAL:_____

TECHNIQUE 1

_____

_____

_____

_____

_____

_____

_____

TECHNIQUE 2

_____

_____

_____

_____

_____

_____

_____

TECHNIQUE 3

_____

_____

_____

_____

_____

_____

_____

NOTES

_____

_____

_____

_____

_____

_____

_____

RATING

1	2	3	4	5	6	7	8	9	10
☐	☐	☐	☐	☐	☐	☐	☐	☐	☐

MINUTES TRAINED: _____

SESSION 49

DATE:_____   BELT RANK:_____

INSTRUCTOR:_____   WEIGHT:_____

TRAINING PARTNERS:_____

SESSION GOAL:_____

TECHNIQUE 1

_____

_____

_____

_____

_____

_____

_____

TECHNIQUE 2

_____

_____

_____

_____

_____

_____

_____

TECHNIQUE 3

_____

_____

_____

_____

_____

_____

_____

NOTES

_____

_____

_____

_____

_____

_____

_____

_____

RATING

1	2	3	4	5	6	7	8	9	10
☐	☐	☐	☐	☐	☐	☐	☐	☐	☐

MINUTES TRAINED: _____

SESSION 50

DATE:_____   BELT RANK:_____

INSTRUCTOR:_____   WEIGHT:_____

TRAINING PARTNERS:_____

SESSION GOAL:_____

TECHNIQUE 1

_____

_____

_____

_____

_____

_____

_____

TECHNIQUE 2

_____

_____

_____

_____

_____

_____

TECHNIQUE 3

_____

_____

_____

_____

_____

_____

_____

NOTES

_____

_____

_____

_____

_____

_____

_____

RATING

1	2	3	4	5	6	7	8	9	10
☐	☐	☐	☐	☐	☐	☐	☐	☐	☐

MINUTES TRAINED: _____

SESSION 51

DATE:_____ BELT RANK:_____

INSTRUCTOR: _____ WEIGHT:_____

TRAINING PARTNERS: _____

SESSION GOAL:_____

TECHNIQUE 1

_____

_____

_____

_____

_____

_____

_____

TECHNIQUE 2

_____

_____

_____

_____

_____

_____

_____

_____

_____

_____

_____

_____

_____

_____

NOTES

_____

_____

_____

_____

_____

_____

_____

RATING

1	2	3	4	5	6	7	8	9	10
☐	☐	☐	☐	☐	☐	☐	☐	☐	☐

MINUTES TRAINED: _____

SESSION 52

DATE:_____   BELT RANK:_____

INSTRUCTOR:_____   WEIGHT:_____

TRAINING PARTNERS:_____

SESSION GOAL:_____

TECHNIQUE 1

_____

_____

_____

_____

_____

_____

_____

TECHNIQUE 2

_____

_____

_____

_____

_____

_____

_____

TECHNIQUE 3

_____

_____

_____

_____

_____

_____

_____

NOTES

_____

_____

_____

_____

_____

_____

_____

RATING

1	2	3	4	5	6	7	8	9	10
☐	☐	☐	☐	☐	☐	☐	☐	☐	☐

MINUTES TRAINED: _____

SESSION 53

DATE:_____   BELT RANK:_____

INSTRUCTOR:_____   WEIGHT:_____

TRAINING PARTNERS: _____

SESSION GOAL:_____

TECHNIQUE 1

_____

_____

_____

_____

_____

_____

_____

TECHNIQUE 2

_____

_____

_____

_____

_____

_____

_____

TECHNIQUE 3

_____

_____

_____

_____

_____

_____

_____

NOTES

_____

_____

_____

_____

_____

_____

_____

RATING

1	2	3	4	5	6	7	8	9	10
☐	☐	☐	☐	☐	☐	☐	☐	☐	☐

MINUTES TRAINED: _____

SESSION 54

DATE:_____   BELT RANK:_____

INSTRUCTOR:_____   WEIGHT:_____

TRAINING PARTNERS: _____

SESSION GOAL:_____

TECHNIQUE 1

_____

_____

_____

_____

_____

_____

_____

TECHNIQUE 2

_____

_____

_____

_____

_____

_____

_____

TECHNIQUE 3

_____

_____

_____

_____

_____

_____

_____

NOTES

_____

_____

_____

_____

_____

_____

_____

RATING

1	2	3	4	5	6	7	8	9	10
☐	☐	☐	☐	☐	☐	☐	☐	☐	☐

MINUTES TRAINED: _____

SESSION 55

DATE:_____ BELT RANK:_____

INSTRUCTOR:_____ WEIGHT:_____

TRAINING PARTNERS:_____

SESSION GOAL:_____

TECHNIQUE 1

_____

_____

_____

_____

_____

_____

_____

TECHNIQUE 2

_____

_____

_____

_____

_____

_____

_____

TECHNIQUE 3

_____

_____

_____

_____

_____

_____

_____

NOTES

_____

_____

_____

_____

_____

_____

_____

RATING

1	2	3	4	5	6	7	8	9	10
☐	☐	☐	☐	☐	☐	☐	☐	☐	☐

MINUTES TRAINED: _____

SESSION 56

DATE:_____   BELT RANK:_____

INSTRUCTOR:_____   WEIGHT:_____

TRAINING PARTNERS:_____

SESSION GOAL:_____

TECHNIQUE 1

_____

_____

_____

_____

_____

_____

_____

TECHNIQUE 2

_____

_____

_____

_____

_____

_____

TECHNIQUE 3

_____

_____

_____

_____

_____

_____

_____

NOTES

_____

_____

_____

_____

_____

_____

_____

RATING

1	2	3	4	5	6	7	8	9	10
☐	☐	☐	☐	☐	☐	☐	☐	☐	☐

MINUTES TRAINED: _____

SESSION 57

DATE:_____   BELT RANK:_____

INSTRUCTOR:_____   WEIGHT:_____

TRAINING PARTNERS: _____

SESSION GOAL:_____

TECHNIQUE 1

_____

_____

_____

_____

_____

_____

_____

TECHNIQUE 2

_____

_____

_____

_____

_____

_____

TECHNIQUE 3

_____

_____

_____

_____

_____

_____

_____

NOTES

_____

_____

_____

_____

_____

_____

_____

RATING

1	2	3	4	5	6	7	8	9	10
☐	☐	☐	☐	☐	☐	☐	☐	☐	☐

MINUTES TRAINED: _____

SESSION 58

DATE:_____   BELT RANK:_____

INSTRUCTOR:_____   WEIGHT:_____

TRAINING PARTNERS:_____

SESSION GOAL:_____

TECHNIQUE 1

_____

_____

_____

_____

_____

_____

_____

TECHNIQUE 2

_____

_____

_____

_____

_____

_____

_____

TECHNIQUE 3

_____

_____

_____

_____

_____

_____

_____

_____

NOTES

_____

_____

_____

_____

_____

_____

_____

_____

RATING

1	2	3	4	5	6	7	8	9	10
☐	☐	☐	☐	☐	☐	☐	☐	☐	☐

MINUTES TRAINED: _____

SESSION 59

DATE:_____   BELT RANK:_____

INSTRUCTOR:_____   WEIGHT:_____

TRAINING PARTNERS:_____

SESSION GOAL:_____

TECHNIQUE 1

_____

_____

_____

_____

_____

_____

_____

TECHNIQUE 2

_____

_____

_____

_____

_____

_____

_____

TECHNIQUE 3

_____

_____

_____

_____

_____

_____

_____

NOTES

_____

_____

_____

_____

_____

_____

_____

RATING

1	2	3	4	5	6	7	8	9	10
☐	☐	☐	☐	☐	☐	☐	☐	☐	☐

MINUTES TRAINED: _____

SESSION 60

DATE:_____   BELT RANK:_____

INSTRUCTOR:_____   WEIGHT:_____

TRAINING PARTNERS:_____

SESSION GOAL:_____

TECHNIQUE 1

_____

_____

_____

_____

_____

_____

_____

TECHNIQUE 2

_____

_____

_____

_____

_____

_____

_____

TECHNIQUE 3

_____
_____
_____
_____
_____
_____
_____

NOTES

_____
_____
_____
_____
_____
_____
_____

RATING

1	2	3	4	5	6	7	8	9	10
☐	☐	☐	☐	☐	☐	☐	☐	☐	☐

MINUTES TRAINED: _____

Manufactured by Amazon.ca
Acheson, AB